Pebble® Plus

Places in Our Community

Our School

by Lisa J. Amstutz

PEBBLE
a capstone imprint

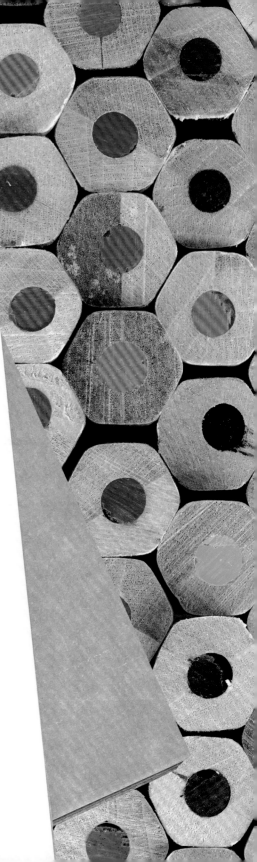

Pebble Plus is published by Pebble, a Capstone imprint.
1710 Roe Crest Drive, North Mankato, Minnesota 56003
www.capstonepub.com

Library of Congress Cataloging-in-Publication data is available on the Library of Congress website.
ISBN 978-1-9771-1263-7 (library binding)
ISBN 978-1-9771-1770-0 (paperback)
ISBN 978-1-9771-1269-9 (eBook PDF)

Summary: Schools are busy places! Lots of community helpers are needed to make a school run smoothly. Readers will learn about who works at a school, what the workers do, and what makes a school special. Simple, at-level text and vibrant photos help readers learn all about schools in the community.

Editorial Credits
Editor: Mari Schuh; Designers: Kay Fraser and Ashlee Suker; Media Researcher: Eric Gohl;
Production Specialist: Katy LaVigne

Photo Credits
Associated Press: St. Louis Post-Dispatch/J.B. Forbes, 15; iStockphoto: FatCamera, 19, Steve Debenport, 13; Zinkevych, 17; Newscom: ZUMA Press/Adolphe Pierre-Louis, 9, ZUMA Press/Elizabeth Flores, 7; Shutterstock: Alexxndr, 2 (notebooks), Betelgejze, 3, Dawn Shearer-Simonetti, cover, HomeArt, 2 (pencils), 23, Leszek Czerwonka, 22, Monkey Business Images, 1, 5, 11, 21, Nadiia Korol, back cover, 4, 6, 8, 10, 12, 14, 16, 18, 20, wavebreakmedia, 24

Note to Parents and Teachers

The Places in Our Community set supports national social studies standards related to people, places, and environments. This book describes and illustrates a school and the people who work there. The images support early readers in understanding the text. The repetition of words and phrases helps early readers learn new words. This book also introduces early readers to subject-specific vocabulary words, which are defined in the Glossary section. Early readers may need assistance to read some words and to use the Table of Contents, Glossary, Read More, Internet Sites, Critical Thinking Questions, and Index sections of the book.

All internet sites appearing in back matter were available and accurate when this book was sent to press.

Printed and bound in China.
002493

Table of Contents

Let's Visit a School!

A school is a busy place!

Kids learn and play there.

Many people work there too.

Let's take a closer look!

Who Works at a School?

High five! The principal greets students. He is the leader of the school. He meets with teachers, students, and parents.

Students walk by the office as they enter the building. An office coordinator signs in visitors. She answers phones and sets up meetings.

The bell rings! A teacher helps students learn. She explains lessons and answers questions. Some teachers teach classes like art or music.

Time to eat! Students hurry to the cafeteria. Cooks make healthy food. They serve it to students. They wash dishes and clean up too.

Oops! Someone made a mess.
The custodian can help
clean up. A custodian keeps
the whole school clean
and safe. Students can help too.

After lunch kids play at recess.

A student hurts her elbow.

She visits the school's nurse.

The nurse cares for students

who are hurt or sick.

After recess students visit
the media center. They find
a media specialist. She reads
to students. She helps them
research and check out books.

Heading Home

Ring! The school day is done.

The students say goodbye.

School is a special place.

It's a place to learn and grow.

Glossary

cafeteria—the room at school where lunch is served

coordinator—a person who organizes people or groups so that they work well together

custodian—a person who maintains a building

information—facts and knowledge

lesson—a set of skills or facts taught at one time; teachers prepare lessons for each day of class

media center—a place with books, magazines, computers, and videos for students to use and borrow

media specialist—someone who works in a school library and helps students find materials and do research

principal—the head of a public school

research—to study and learn about a subject

Read More

Bullard, Lisa. *Who Works at Hannah's School?* Minneapolis: Millbrook Press, 2018.

Gaertner, Meg. *Teachers.* Minneapolis: Pop!, a division of Abdo, 2019.

Weakland, Mark. *This Is My School.* North Mankato, MN.: Picture Window Books, a Capstone imprint, 2019.

Internet Sites

Fact Monster: Teachers
https://www.factmonster.com/cool-stuff/jobs-involving-helping-people/teacher

Community Helpers Worksheet
https://www.enchantedlearning.com/alphabet/alphabeticalorder/themes/10communityhelperwords/

Community Club: Librarian
http://teacher.scholastic.com/commclub/librarian/

Critical Thinking Questions

1. What is a school nurse's job?

2. List two ways media specialists help students.

3. Name two other workers who help students at school.

4. How can students help school workers during the school day?

Index